ELECTRICITY

SCIENCE SECRETS

Jason Cooper

Rourke

Publishing LLC

Vero Beach, Florida 32964

www.rourkepublishing.com

PHOTO CREDITS: Title page, page 6 © South Dakota Dept. of Tourism; page 13, © Painet, Inc.; pages 4, 10, 17, 18 © K-8 Images; page 12 © Corbis Images; pages 18, 15, 21 © Jerry Hennen; pages

Title page: *A spectacular lightning storm*

Series Editor: Henry Rasof

Cover and interior design by Nicola Stratford

Library of Congress Cataloging-in-Publication Data

Cooper, Jason, 1942-
  Electricity / Jason Cooper.
      p. cm. — (Science secrets)
Summary: Provides a simple discussion of natural and man-made electricity and of how electrical power is generated and used. Includes bibliographical references and index.
  ISBN 1-58952-410-1 (hardcover)
  1. Electricity—Juvenile literature. [1. Electricity.] I. Title. II.
  Series: Cooper, Jason, d 1942- Science secrets.
  QC527.2 .C67 2002
  537—dc21
                                        2002015701

Printed in the USA

TABLE OF CONTENTS

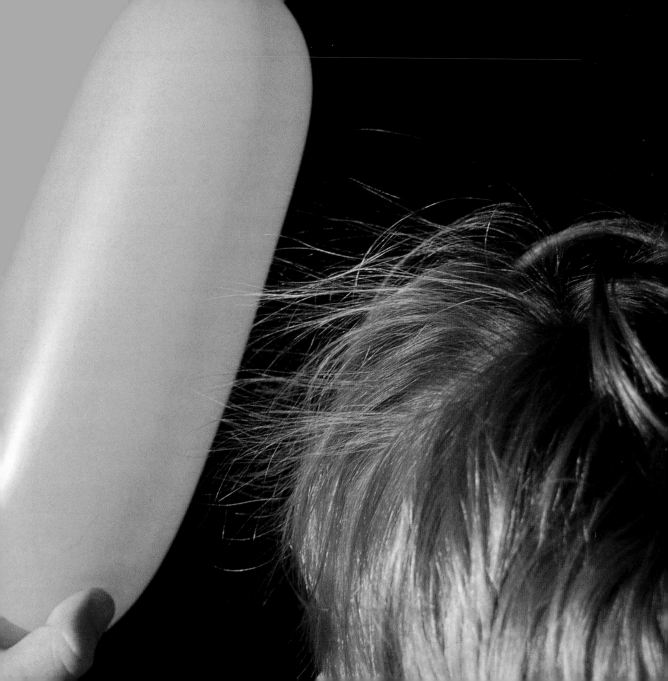

A TYPE OF ENERGY

Electricity is one type of **energy**, or power. Although we think of electricity as being contained in wires, electricity is actually all around us. Electricity is even in our bodies and in other living things.

By controlling the electricity around us, we are making electricity work for us. We are changing the world.

Rubbing a balloon on your hair causes friction, which creates static electricity..

ELECTRICITY IN NATURE

Everything in our world is made up of tiny invisible pieces called **particles**. One type of particle is the **electron**. Power is created by moving millions of electrons. This power is electricity.

Electrons that move in thunderclouds form electric **current**. This current makes huge sparks, which are flashes of lightning.

Lightning is an electric current in the sky.

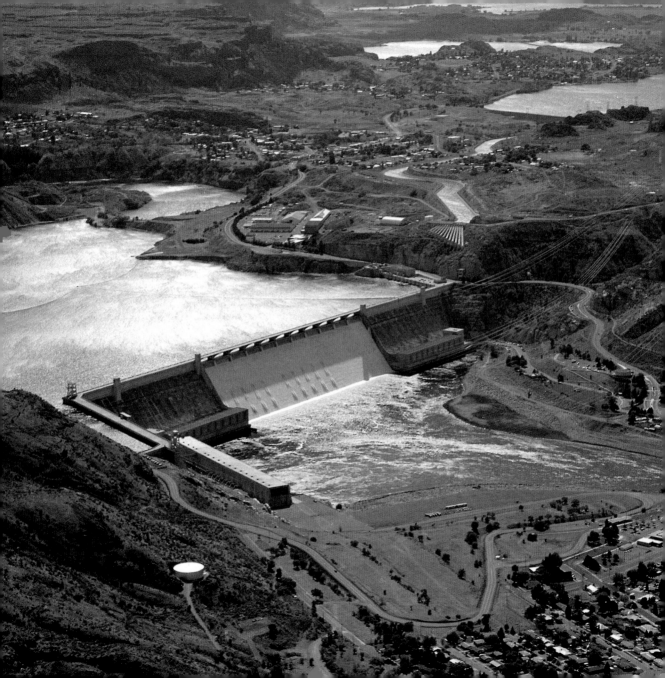

MAKING ELECTRICITY

People can also create electricity. They do this at electric power stations. Machines known as **generators** make electricity. They do this by using other forms or sources of energy, including coal, falling water, wind, gas, oil, and atomic energy.

A generator pushes electrons into wires as a flow, or current, of electricity. Wires are known as **conductors** because they conduct, or carry, an electric current.

Water is often used to create electricity.

SENDING ELECTRICITY

Electricity travels through conductors to homes, factories, and many other places. It enters your home through wires made of metal, usually copper or aluminum. Metal is a good conductor.

You can control the flow of electricity with switches that turn it on or off. When you turn a light switch off, you turn off the electricity. The light goes out.

These electric power lines bring electricity to our homes.

Computers need electricity to work.

Electricity brings power to model train layouts.

ELECTRICITY'S POWER

Watch a bolt of lightning as it streaks across the sky. It may strike the ground, or it may not. Lightning that strikes a power line can cause the power to go out. The amount of electric power in lightning is huge. And we cannot control this power.

But we can control the electricity made in power stations. It is forced into wires. And like lightning, the electricity produces heat, power, and light.

Power stations carry electricity to our homes.

USING ELECTRICITY

We use electricity in our homes, offices, schools, and labs. Electricity lights our buildings and often cooks our food. It also powers many kinds of machines. Telephones, computers, and televisions are all powered by electricity.

Electricity has helped bring people in different countries closer together.

Electricity is used to cook our food.

"TAKE-OUT" ELECTRICITY

How do people get electricity when they are away from home or work? They use "take-out" electricity from a **battery**.

Batteries are usually containers filled with **chemicals** and metal. The action that takes place between the metal and the chemicals makes electricity. Batteries help power cameras, computers, trains, radios, toys, and many other devices.

Batteries come in many different sizes and shapes.

ELECTRICITY AND SAFETY

Electricity is very powerful. Signs that say "High Voltage" mean that strong electric currents are present. Electricity can be a friend or an enemy. A jolt of electricity is known as an electric shock. It can hurt or even kill someone. Do not touch electric devices if your hands or feet are wet.

Remember that lightning is a kind of electricity. Stay inside or in a vehicle with a hard top when there is lightning.

A broken power line can change soil into glass.

PIONEERS IN ELECTRICITY

In 1752 Benjamin Franklin used a kite to prove that lightning was electricity. But people did not use electricity as a light source until a little more than 100 years ago. In 1882 the famous inventor Thomas Alva Edison began a small electric company in New York City. He was able to offer electric lights to just 400 customers! Today, people in most parts of the world use electricity.

GLOSSARY

battery (BAH ter ee) — an object made of metal and chemicals that make electricity

chemicals (KEM uh kulz) — a substance obtained by a chemical process

conductors (kun DUCK turz) — things that carry, or conduct, such as a copper wire that conducts electricity

current (KER unt) — the flow, or ongoing passage of something, such as the flow of electrons

electron (ee LEK tron) — one of the invisible pieces, or particles, in the natural make-up of all things

energy (EN ur jee) — power; the ability to do work

generators (JEN er ay turz) — machines that make, or produce, electric power

particles (PAR tuh kulz) — tiny, invisible pieces of matter, such as electrons

Index

Further Reading

Berger, Melvin. *Switch on, Switch off*. New York: HarperCollins, 2001.
Simon, Seymour. *Lightning*. New York: Morrow, 1997.
Tocci, Salvatore. *Experiments with Electricity*. Danbury, CT: Children's Press, 2001.

Websites To Visit

ippex.pppl.gov/interactive/electricity/
www.howstuffworks.com/category-electronics.htm
www.energyquest.ca.gov/scientists/edison.html
www.energyquest.ca.gov/scientists/franklin.html

About The Author

Jason Cooper has written several children's book series about a variety of topics for Rourke Publishing, including *Eye to Eye with Big Cats* and *Money Power*. Cooper travels widely to gather information for his books.